HAGGARDS

ALSO BY ELIZABETH RIMMER

Wherever We Live Now (Red Squirrel Press, 2011)
The Territory of Rain (Red Squirrel Press, 2015)

Haggards

ELIZABETH RIMMER

Poems

RED SQUIRREL PRESS

First published in 2018 by Red Squirrel Press
www.redsquirrelpress.com

Designed and typeset by Gerry Cambridge
www.gerrycambridge.com

Cover image: Olga Korneeva/Shutterstock.com

A CIP catalogue record is available from the British Library.

ISBN: 978 1 910437 61 2

Red Squirrel Press is committed to a sustainable future. This book
is printed in the UK by Imprint Digital using Forest Stewardship
Council certified paper.

Contents

❧ Wild-Crafted ❧

Haggards

These are the places in between,
between the field and the mountain,
between the cattle and the sheep,
between the orchard and the road,
between the heather and the sea,

places where growth is curbed
by salt, or drought or altitude,
by rocks beneath, by standing water,
by wind, by fire, by lawlessness,

places for forgotten things, and things
no longer valued, the weeds and black bees,
the wrens and thrawn roots of Latin
the boys were taught in secret.

These are the places in between,
too small for the rich to care for,
where things grow stronger for neglect,
where questions thrive, and dreams, cut down
to the roots, grow hardy, come back strong.

Cora's Garden

—for Cora Greenhill

When all this is over,
and the sun moves casually on
from the flat vertiginous
stone of your garden,
darkness will hide the cat
threading the jungle of ivy.
Mice will replace blue tits,
foraging for dropped seeds.
Stars will shine in the blue
over the gleaming frosted rails.

When all this is over
and all the people have gone home,
when the music stops, and *gyil*
and *mbiri* are back in the box,
the book you launched tonight
will make its persistent way
downriver to a sea of poems
through letter boxes and reviews.

When all this is over,
trains caught, bags unpacked,
and you and I are back
beside our separate hearths,
the roots of new work
will strike into the subsoil
of friendship and send up shoots,
twined and tangled and leafy,
rich and fertile as ivy.

Grassroots in the Meadows

—for Katherine Cameron

There's so much surprising green in this city's
grey stone heart, so douce, so mercantile.
I miss that four-pointed arch at Jawbone Walk
beyond the cherry trees, all pink and lyrical
under a wide spring sky, enormous, shocking
in its frank commemoration of brutality,
yet this is generous. There are paths here
for cyclists and joggers and grass for barbeques,
teens making out, students with their books,
but no-one selling anything but thought—
all this space and no ice-cream concession,
but campaign booths and vegan festivals
and summer camps for children, rainbow flags.
Radical starts here, with all the marches—
stop climate change, ban Trident, the white
ribbon we wrapped round Edinburgh
to make poverty history. It's the place for change,
beyond the university's bounds. I saw
my first feminist badge here—*the future is female*—
pink on the coat of a mother at the swings.
But most radical of all, on that March day
before Thatcher, in the winter of discontent,
when snow fell, and lay, and froze, and people
skied down Princes Street, we put on hiking boots
and crossed the Meadows to the Simpson,
last day of two, the day when you were born.

The Skye Stone

I hold a stone from Skye,
sharp-edged, and ridged
like its mother mountain,
white and grey-speckled.
I found it in the Quiraing
where the bitter sky
was wide enough for eagles
and the wind was cold.
Here was more than a view,
a backdrop to memory.
I stood in a kist of light
holding all of Scotland
cupped in my open hands.

The Scent of Winter

A drift of cinnamon and pine
from candles in the mall clings
to my clothes. Frost sparkles
like the bite of static on my skin.
Into the silver evening my ghost
strides out in front of me,
over the South Bridge and into
a past of infinite promise.

Maquis

Cicada is the song of the sun,
this metal-grinding electrical
racket, louder than traffic,
and constant. It hammers
the hillsides, greedy, relentless,
seizing the burning day.

Rock is a crucible for silvered
downy leaves, sharp stems,
volatile oils that will suppress
competing growth, the scent
and sudden fires. There's ash
and charcoal, parching thirst.

The hill is stripped by goats,
impoverished by vineyards.
The wine they make,
and honey gathered here
will taste of herbs and limestone,
strength and stubbornness.

Post Industrial

Two quarry pools
dark water under a sheer cliff
gold floating birch leaves

In childhood gardens, upturned
green hulls of andersen shelters
used for spades and motor bikes,
dusty lilacs, ash heaps,
goldenrod and flowering currant.

On brownfield mining sites
thin, low-nutrient soils
no growth of rich and dominant plants—
untidy and unnatural
greening slag-heaps
priority habitats.

Harsh sodium light
pollutes the night sky.
The stars are lost, and dreams
come more rarely, the glare
of one kind of knowledge
crowding out another.

Scouring

Things get scoured when my life goes wrong—
my mother's teaspoons, when she was ill,
a copper tray I polished till my hands were black
before your father's funeral, the cobwebs
from behind the radiator. Things were scrubbed,
oiled and mended, folded and ironed.
Things were put away then, and never again after.
Today I have washed the dressing gown
that hung behind the door, and the large black shawl
you brought from India. These small acts of making good
divert me from what's underneath our house—
tectonic shifts, small falls and stresses in the faith
we've had in weather, honesty, the common will
to kindness, your solid presence in my life.

Beltane

—i.m. Eleanor Murray

Although it was that other fire-time,
October, when you died, now
is when I best remember you,
the time for cleaning, bringing in the light,
chucking out the debris, making new.

Happiest when you made life over—
moving to the cottage on the Carse,
planting the new garden—you cut loose
from habit and old grief, brought in the light.
It was so short, that time, so short.

That vinca, which you gave me, and I still call
Ellie's double blue, is flowering yet,
and I keep still that note stuck on your door,
more true than funny, as things turned out,
saying you were (really) out to lunch.

The Uses of Nostalgia

You look into the fire, and dream of home—
the mingled smell of lemongrass and bleach.
It has become unbearable, the loss
of something dim, less loved than longed for.
You crave your mother's baking. She never baked.

You hang the trees with bunting, learn to knit,
make jam, pick ransoms, stitch the quilts
your Granny made and hated. Now you save
the seeds of plants your father weeded out.
You blacklead grates. Your stock is made from scratch.

It feels like fantasy, this flowery pastel nest,
kept far from politics and poverty alike,
but something else is stirring here, a cry of pain,
a knowledge of which battles must be fought,
and what the heart most needs, to take them on.

El Duende

Grief lives in my house
like dry rot infesting the timbers.
It has taken up residence
in the cellar, where I do not go.
I pretend there is no such space.
But he sits there, smoking coltsfoot tobacco,
and brewing a bitter tisane
of rue and wormwood, hyssop and dill.
Too much indulgence, he says,
in sweet things like joy and kindness,
all the fruit of sunlight and fresh rain,
have done me harm.
It is time to take my medicine,
time for a purge, a cleansing.
Hell mend ye, he says. And hope.

Schoolish

The things which you learn with your hands,
your tongue, your ears, the glimpses
at the edge of vision, are not the things
we want you to write down.
The things you learn by mixing, heating
breaking, stirring and waiting
are not of interest here. The things
you feel, or come to understand
in a leaf-fall, a bird flight, a sharp
look between two people on a bench
in the sun before one of them leaves,
you should keep to yourself. In this book
we write the proper names, and instructions,
copying carefully, respecting the authorities.
Marks will be lost for poor handwriting,
spelling, grammar and demotic vocabulary.
Draw your conclusions. Make quite sure
they are the right ones. Try not to care.

Who Knows

—for Ginny Battson

There are people who know the world
in specifics—not gull, but black-backed,
(lesser and greater), black-headed,
common, glaucous and herring.

There are people who know the woods—
not trees, but oak, willow, hazel,
aspen, and lime, and not oak
but sessile or pedunculate.

There are people who learn the names,
the Latin, the genus, the cultivar,
making lists for countries and years,
and the life-list with the bbjs,
the ticks, and the gaps they need to fill.

And then, there are other people
whose hands and eyes know everything,
who taste the wind for salt or coming rain,
who find the right leaf, or root, or berry
for health or flavour, without a word spoken.

There are people who know their gardens
like their family, their lawn like their own skin,
a new bird by the frisson the cat makes,
even before the stranger's call
breaks into the grey still morning.

And who can tell us which of these
knows best, knows more, can teach,
protect or harvest earth and sky
and water for the common good?

Or shall we try for both, a lore
of senses, heart and mind at one,
where knowledge and compassion
are held in equal balance, equal trust?

A Poem Is

A poem is an arrow flight.
A poem is a picklock,
  a scavenger in other people's sorrows.
A poem is a map with a warning—
  'Here be dragons.'
A poem can be played
  in all the three musics.
A poem is a doctor's letter
  a diagnosis, an appointment with honesty.
A poem is a window.
A poem is an artesian well, a bomb.
A poem is a satnav.
A poem is a bubble of amber
  and in it, a chimaera.
A poem is restless, a hunter,
  a heat-seeking missile.
A poem is a song heard in a lift,
  which you can't identify or get out of your head.
A poem is not an excuse,
  a poultice, a call to arms.
A poem is whatever we allow it to be.

Voice

An instrument tuned
by the precise small tensions
of muscle in tongue and lips and throat,
the flow of breath and spit.

The Occupation of Poetry

—for the Federation of Writers (Scotland)

A bench on a strip of grass, hemmed in
by bramble, sallow, hawthorn and mud.
Someone has planted a wild flower verge,
cutting into the sward of plantain, daisy
and wild clover, mowing off the willowherb
and meadowsweet, to sow new seeds
of foil-bright poppies, cornflowers, brassy
yellow corn marigolds. For bees, they said.
Dock and dandelion colonised the strip.
Thistledown blew in soft clouds, set seeds
between the battered wet stems. The birds,
bees and hoverflies carried on, the way
they had for years. This place did not need
permission or instruction to nurture its own.
It had a story of its own, already under way.
Sit for a while and listen, put down roots here.
Its story will be part of yours. Then write.

The Revolution Will Not Be Crowd-Funded

The revolution will not be engineered.
Someone with a hammer will casually
construct the new homes out of the wreck
of burned-out shopping malls.

The revolution will not be forecast.
It will happen in small outbreaks
and daily resistance to the dull
and casual cruelties of power, to build
stout bulwarks of compassion.

The revolution will not be fertilised.
It will happen in despite
of good intentions, celandines
seeding through the cracks
in broken tarmac or the stillness
of abandoned airfields.

The revolution will not be smart,
specific, measurable or timed.
The heart will have its way, and love
will be ineluctable as lightning
in a clear sky, arcing everywhere.

Stand in the Light

Stand in the light.
Allow the wild things to creep
out of the shadows.
Welcome them all, the wet
bedraggled things, the ones
all spit and claws, the one
who weeps and hangs its head,
the one who stares, and says, 'Make me.'
Stand in the light. They are yours,
washed and unwashed alike.

Stand in the light, and sing.
Raise your voice as if
there was no fear of darkness.
Listen and you will hear
other voices, other songs,
rough and sweet and dauntless,
blues and *canto jondo*,
pibroch, *nanha, tanakh*.
Stand in the light and sing. Their pain
is yours. Allow it to hurt.

Stand in the light. Be still.
Light is what we need. Let it glow,
let it shine into the furthest dark
to find the lost forgotten hopes
and warm them to new life.
Allow it to grow and touch the ruined
homes and hearts and show us
what's to mend. Stand in the light.
Be still. Become the light.

✹ Materia Medica ✹

Dreaming of Herb Gardens

It is morning now and you
are in your own house. Sun
has melted the frost and birds
are already building nests.

Downstairs the woman
who wears her hair like leaves,
has mud on her boots and grass
on the torn hem of her skirt

has left, and there's an open door.
The smell of fox and wet earth blends
with homely oranges and coffee.
Slug tracks glint on the mat.

She haunts you, that possible self,
a wise earth mother, whose pots
run over with good food, medicine,
dyes for hand spun wool, or soap.

There's comfort in that channelled woman
who knows her place, seductive
as Circe, but nurturing, her power
contained in that small scented realm.

There's glamour there, the lure
of home, an art-nouveau dream
of flowing skirts, long hair,
a voice of power, though gentle,

glimpsed firesides, the feel of magic
in the dim cave of your house,
archetypal, and nothing like
this daily cold wet earth,

these mildewed leaves,
this new shoot bursting
from a withered stem,
this scent, this bitter taste,

this growing life.

A Charm of Nine Haggard Herbs

We are nine, a triple trinity
of leaf and flower and fruit,
a gift to blood and bone and breath.

Elder is first, the gift of summer,
white flowers to clear the skin
and banish cold from heart and lungs.

Hawthorn is home to birds and fairies.
Its flowers smell of death, but its berry
is good to strengthen heart and veins.

Though yarrow's flower is small and dull,
its feathery leaf is used for staunching wounds,
its bitterness heals and mends the skin.

Clover, beloved of bees and sweet
as a loved girl's footprints, is remedy
for coughs, and quickens growing plants.

Comfrey, with its deep roots, its strong
leaf growth, mends bones, and brings up
deep-lying minerals in the soil.

Dandelion, the piss-a-bed kidney herb,
has power to cleanse, to bring down
the over-mighty, encourage what is sluggish.

Wild rose, bright baubles on its thorny stem
for winter sweetness, calm, and strength
against fevers and grief of heart.

Plantain is used to clear poison. Rub the leaf
to soothe the bites and stings of insects.
It is so low underfoot, yet mighty.

Bramble, a tangle of thorn, and things
that buzz and sting, its dark and glowing
berries are the joy of autumn.

We are nine, we are closer than you think
in the wild and unregarded places in between.
We are haggard, and we survive.

The Doctrine of Signatures

Those white spots on the leaf are signs,
says William Cole, who dislikes astrology,
of a plant for the healing of lungs.
He sees signs everywhere. Red spots
on leaves of St. John's wort, when held
against the sun, appear like pores,
and thus, the herb will heal the skin.
Tuberous roots of embarrassing shape
he tells us, are appropriately known
as pilewort. Those veins so prominent
on a plantain leaf mean health for heart
and blood. Yellow flowers clear jaundice.
Heart-shaped petals on rose or violet
will tell you what it's good for.
No medicinal plant without its sign,
God-given, he says, unlike the foolish claims
of other doctors, missing the useful habit
of those who learn, to create a hook
for memory, for passing wisdom on.

The Curse of Horsetails

Like horrible Christmas trees, a bristly
foot-high net of pure silica, horsetails
reproach the gardener. Their black
roots thread the wet ground, invade
neglected gardens, remind us by their
dull persistence that they were here,
with ferns and moss, before the trees
and dinosaurs. They will not succumb
to hoes and competition.
They mean to outlive us all.

Spindle-Tree

Arrowy leaves, dull crimped white flowers
until the summer's done, and then a blaze
of pink and orange, molten red and bronze,
a hedgerow bonfire of leaf and fruit—
this is the spinner's tree, the dyer's tree,
the tree that spangles the humdrum
with softness, warmth, and colour.
It ought to be exotic, its flaming leaves,
its tri-lobed fruit, bright pink and glowing
like a Christmas bauble, but it's not.
This is no grace and favour tenancy,
no feral wanderer beyond its bounds,
it's native, it belongs in this wild space
here, like art, like passion, like the joy
in work that makes us rich and free.

The Herb for Nightmares

I might sing of Hymettus, the honey mountain,
the Crazy Mountain, where the bees
are all mad for it, brawling and sprawling
over the pink flower-cushions of thyme.

I might sing of the honey, pouring like amber
into the jars, tasting of flowers and resin,
of pepper, dates, cloves, and smelling
of burned plastic and pencils.

I might sing of its neat green leaves like pins,
its creeping unassuming habit, its familiar
scent and savour, its kitchen-haunting
presence in all we cook with meat.

I might sing of its woody stems, simmered
in water for disinfectant, smelling
of health and cleanliness, piercing
the clog and slow drain of colds.

I might sing of maidens embroidering
the furious black bees on thyme sprays,
whose fierce strength brought ardour
to the knights who wore their favours.

But I will choose to sing of the quiet
comfort thyme brings to those who suffer
with 'phrensie and lethargie,' its peace for those
whose sleep is plagued with nightmares.

That's for Remembrance

*Stand by the roads, and look, and ask for the ancient
paths, where the good way is; and walk in it, and find
rest for your souls. (Jeremiah 6:16)*

The scent is of pine and salt and summer,
the tang of barbeque and olive oil,
and the resinous bristly leaves
hiding the small pale early flowers.

Remember how things used to be,
when the children were small
or we were young, and everything
was still ahead and full of hope.

Remember that we once made time
for friends, and had ideals, and talked
with passion late at night about how
we wanted just to make things right.

Take a breath, and smell the rosemary.
Let it clear your mind, go back.

Hyssop for Repentance

This is the herb for a place of pain.
Its bitter tang is tonic for indulgence,
its blue bee-bothered flower tips
cleansing, dispersing phlegm and clotted blood,
old grief and lingering remorse.
Sprinkled with water from a hyssop twig,
the sufferer is purified and purged.
Something dies, an old life, an old poison—
and something flies free, forever gone.
The space is clear. Time to start again.

The Lifting of Melancholy

Balm for bees, with its honeyed Latin name,
melissa, and its green crumpled fans,
its white flowered spires, its lemon scented breath.
Balm for breakfast with honey, to extend
the life of princes, and for Carmelites,
a sweet scent for baths and laundered linen.

Balm the roisterer, its spring exuberance
spreading lax between the sage and parsley,
a hang-out for cuckoo spit and blackfly,
and dulled by August to fading tatters.
It spits its myriad black pinheads of seeds
casually, wherever it likes, all over the plot.

Balm for hurting minds, for headaches,
dejected spirits and worn out hearts,
balm for the lifting of melancholy,
a tea to comfort the stomach, ease fevers,
clean old wounds and restore lost youth—
lemon balm, bringer of joy.

Bring Always Courage

The borage stem is both soft and spiky,
bristles sharp enough to scratch an eyeball
but melting in the mouth to cold
astringent taste of cucumber.
You'd put it in a cooling drink
to bring mirth, to comfort the heart.
The stem shatters to straight stiff fibres
under a careless foot, but its sinuous curves,
too long for its girth, too heavy for its brittle
thready stalk, stretch through the border.
Its blue, black-whiskered flowers
are star-shaped cups of something
bumble bees adore, in which they wallow
with a strange metallic purring,
falling onto the grass, drunk on summer.

Lime Flower

Leaves drip from her outspread fingers
quivering in summer's warm
west wind, because she is last in leaf.
She flowers, a spray of feathered
ear-rings, suspended from long bracts
as slim as pencil shavings,
and swinging in the hum of bee-
traffic in the dappled glinting
underwater cave of summer.
Sunlight mingles with chlorophyll,
soft movement, gentle obsessive
humming, bringing peace to calm
a sulking bowered poet, and soothing
tea for chills and fractious children.
Leaf-fall and winter leave her
still and statuesque, a perfect arch,
sculptural and stately, hoarding the rain.

The Helmet of Jupiter

—'*Jupiter claims this herb*'
Nicholas Culpepper Herbal

Sage is his, he says, this blue helmet-shaped flower
Set *on vertillicim*, in spikes, with its clammy *calices*,
its four round seeds held in the hollow *galea*,
its powerful scent, its warming oil.

It quickens the senses, he says, restoring
memory and ease and lightness of heart.
It is an old man's herb, good for the bones
and cold lingering headaches. Why should
a man die if he grows sage in his garden?

And yet it will only grow in a garden
where the woman is in charge. Jupiter
may claim it, but surely it is Juno who grows
this wonder-working herb, this remedy
for old age, this botanical wisdom?

Queen of the Meadows

Much I do not envy them—the cold houses,
the meat-heavy banquets and bread like stone,
haphazard medicine, and tolerance of fleas,
mice, dogs under the table, and violent men
drunk by bedtime. But meadowsweet,
gathered in the summer and strewn
among the rushes when floors were swept—
this I love. The curds and cream handfuls
of blossom, the flossy stamens, like flecks
of ripening butter, and sunlight burning crimson
in the stems against the hedgerow's deep green,
its scent of honey, freshness in stale air,
comfort in the aches of winter—this I would choose
for my house. A herb for the merry of heart.

Lady's Mantle

I have seen it on the hills of Argyll,
beside waterfalls in Iceland, in the machair
of the islands, its pleated fans scalloped
like a petticoat, cupped to hold the dew,
and magical, they say, this dew a crystal
for scrying the future, a lotion to wash the face
on Mayday. Its root is edible, and it seeds
like dandelions, gripping the cold ground,
resilient to cold and wind and wet.
And yet, in kinder gardens it grows lush,
its leaves full and generous, and its flowers
yellow-green as absinthe, foaming like lace
in the dappled queenly shade of roses.

Instructions to the Laundrymaid

If you boil your sheets in summer
with well-dried roots of orris,
in winter, they will be perfumed
with the fleeting scent of violets.
Imagine the oven, fired all day
with wood for bread, cakes and pies,
drying wet boots and feathers for pillows,
full coppers of water drawn from the well
boiling all day, and laundry
hot-washed, cold rinsed, blued
and hung to dry, sun-bleached
and flat-ironed, laid among lavender—
the love, the labour, the pride
in doing a hard job well. It took a week.
She did it twice a year.

Molly-blobs

In the cold dips, the damp hollows
where clay holds the winter wet,
there are fires of gold, bright blobs
of buttery yellow, spreading wide petals
to early bees, calling back the sun.
All their medicine is magical,
but potent, nonetheless.
Their power keeps the good folk
from the cattle, makes the butter
come rich and soft, and colours
the dye pots, gilding the tweed.

Iris

Once I made a boat
from the thin spear of iris leaf,
a slit along the central vein,
the supple tip bent, pushed through
to form a blown-out sail,
a flat vertical for mast,
a keel and pointed centreboard
for balance, a toy for childhood.

Later it was a plant I longed
to draw, to make it mine—
loving how its buttery bright falls
way-marked for entering bees,
disclose the up-curled standards
gold flames in the green dips where rain
soaks the sullen grasping clay.

It's red-listed now, grown scarce
since land is prized for houses—
the yellow flag, a messenger,
of blended light and water
in outposts of neglected land.

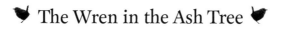 The Wren in the Ash Tree

Prologue: The Bird Who Brought the Fire

The birds have come back to the garden,
second brood starlings and sparrows
lined up along hedges, combing the lawn's thatch
for spilt grass seeds, emerging ants. Blue tits
cling to whippy branches, dunnocks pry into cracks
in the bark, goldfinches pick apart seed heads
of nettle and marigold. A willow warbler slips
furtive between the stiff dulling birch leaves
and blackbirds plunder the ripening currants.
The last swifts scythe the hot air, quilted
with sulk and threat of storm. The cormorant's
black crossbow looms above, heavy with hunger
and this year's wren sings on a high branch
claiming in summer his winter territory.
El Niño has exhaled a great hot sigh.
The ice is melting, sliding off Greenland's cliffs
into seas blooming with plankton. There are storms
and flash floods, blight and failure of crops.
There is drought in Africa and famine and war.
But the wren is on his high perch singing.
The druid's bird, the bard's bird, shaman's bird,
Brigid's chicken, the mouse's brother,
sits on his high perch and cries out, so loud
a voice in his small breast 'Now! Now! Now!'

Canto 1: The Outcry

The hanging man says,
'Outcry of grief
goes up and down the world-tree,
grumble of ravens and chattering classes
in tweets and rumours on smartphones.
Her leaves are nibbled by squirrels,
in curtained bedrooms and behind
the facades of abandoned shops,
browsed to the bark by greedy stags,
in city suits and plate-glassed offices
her roots undermined by serpents
wasting the soil. The hedges are down,
the fenlands drained and the red dust
is washed off suburban car fronts.'

The wren is singing in the bramble bush.

The woman at the ford says,
'On one bank of the river,
there is a lament for the fallen,
on the other, the outcry
of those who have lost everything,
and there is never enough
of blood or tears.'

El duende says,
'This is the place of pain.
To sing here you will need
to open the heart,
the lungs and voice,
and meet it square.
You can't sing from hiding,
nor drunk or afraid.
You can't sing this softly
like chocolate in the sun.

You must give yourself
to the fight with all your strength.
It will take all you've got.
It will feel like death.'

The wren slips between the branches
of the birch tree without a sound.

And the field says,
'You can't write my music.
There ain't no sixteen bars,
no twelve bar phrases here—
field music comes bursting
straight from the heart.'

The city is silent.
All the roundabouts
are wearing flowers
dressed in cellophane
and there are soft toys
on every doorstep.

The song from the city is sung
behind a proscenium arch,
in other voices, not ours,
and we are shamed by silence.

The wren is hidden
among the leaves of the ash
and sings without ceasing.

And the *púca* sings
in the depths of the sea,
'The water is poisoned with oil
and the krill are scarce. We are hungry

and choking on plastic.
There are small boats, sinking
beneath the weight of sorrow
and the men with guns who turn
the lost ones away from their coasts.'

And the völva is casting the runes.
The leather bag is thick,
tough and unbending,
and gives away no secrets,
but the stones mutter
and grind against each other.
The black angular lines—
tree, hammer, wealth,
ocean, ice—will come together,
fall in the right configuration,
give their bleak verdict soon enough.

The rune for harvest is the same
as the rune for the day of reckoning.

And the wren sings on the bare branches,
sings without ceasing.

Canto 2: Fuga Mundi

What do you do when the earth is stolen
from under your feet? What do you do when
the landlord says your rent isn't enough,
so you can't stay where your grandfathers
lived and died? where your children
were born, under weather you understand?
Where do you go when the sea boils
and the rocks shudder with the weight
of destruction raining from planes
belonging to people you never heard of?

Where do you go when the job is killing you
and you never see your children and your pay
is gone from your bank account before
you have thought how to spend it?
You ask yourself, 'Why pay money
for what is not bread?' And you ask yourself
the price of sleep.

Where do you go when the water is poisoned
with salt or nitrate, or when the mud is inches deep
in your kitchen and the rain has not stopped for a week?

Wrens are hiding from bitter weather
deep in the cracks between stones
huddled together for warmth in a space
smaller than you would think possible.

When the nights are dark and open-eyed you dream
of building the last homely house, an ark,
a treasury for all that is going to be lost.
In the centrally-heated houses the people
are dreaming of a life off-grid, of growing their own,
of communities made over, honest and kindly,
where there is welcome for the stranger,

but nobody comes, because everyone
has a home of their own, and the sick are healed,
but no-one gets sick, because the air is clean
and the life is so healthy. There will be orchards
and bees and chickens, and the laughter
of children in sunlit meadows, and fires
on the hearth, and time for songs.
All you need is the land, you say,
but who owns the land?

Who owns the land? Who owns the seeds?
And where does the water come from?
How did we get so ignorant? and who
will teach us now, how to live
without waste, without breaking the earth,
without so much fear, without despair?
Who can we trust to tell us
the truth in a time of trouble?

This place is done, broken and worn out.
We need somewhere else, somewhere new,
clean and unspoiled. And there is no such place.

A wren flits over the frost-hard ground,
mouse-brown, mouse-quiet and the eye
of the hawk does not see him.

Canto 3: There Are Lights

'Every Woman a Signal Tower '
Ciara Phillips, The Dazzle Ship Project

This is my own landscape—the hollow ways,
the feminine curves of grasslands,
small rivers, willow trees,
hedges of elder and hawthorn,
a stealth of dunnock and whitethroat
in the honeysuckle and wild rose
tangling the young ash trees.

The wren is safe here, it can swim,
it will forage under the snow.
It is the lady of heaven's chicken
and must not be harmed
or eaten, because it lives,
men say, on spiders and poison.

The air is cold towards dusk, and
the quiet lanes and curtained homes
are haunted by grief and rage,
isolation, poverty, loss and fear.
But in the gloom there are lights
shining as women kindle fires,
put lamps in windows, look out
for the lost, the returning family,
the friends in need of shelter.
Each writing, cooking, walking,
protesting woman is a signal tower,
creates a net to catch us when we fall.

I know a woman who studies the brains of owls,
their neural networks so fine, so fast,
their signals unimpeded by noisy spikes,
transistor mismatch. The smallest,

finest signals flow through the chips
she builds. She works for women in science
to come together, find their place made stronger.

I knew a woman who got things done—
teachers taught new skills, girls given chances,
children taken out of doors to learn and play—
her days at Greenham Common,
her voice at meetings remembered
as she made her last demands,
time running out, 'More rigorous data,
more commitment, more bloody vision!'
In her memory, women
will learn to stand straight, walk tall.

The wren sits on the garden fence.
His song is loud, ecstatic, not to claim
his territory, but to call a mate. He sings
because she visits the nest he built.

I knew a woman who lived at home.
It fell to her, a telephone operator
in war-time when the small neat hands
of women were valued at the exchange,
to write the letters bonding scattered families—
the brothers gone to sea, an aunt away
down south, a sister on the missions.
She filled the thin blue air-mail forms
kept ready in the sideboard drawer
with small news of mother's health,
or children gone to school, a neighbour dead,
in her looped careful handwriting,
so neat, so regular, so hard to read.
Her letters crossed the world
a quiet regular pulse of love—
'my dear Frank, my dear Jim,
my dear Betty'—I feel it still.

But who will now praise famous women?
A valiant woman who will find her?
Who will remember Joanna Macy,
Elizabeth Warren, Mhairi Black,
Josephine Bacon, Malala Yousafzai,
our own Mary Barbour, Dorothy Stang,
Wangari Maathai, Berta de Caceres,
Big Mary Morrison of the Songs,
or Mary Brooksbank of Dundee?
These are women whose signals rang
through poetry and politics, songs
and planted forests, women whose voices
cried out for the poor, for democracy,
for the life of women, for the earth.

And who will praise the women in their millions
who walked in pink hats, under rainbow flags
on January twenty-first, on seven continents,
and not one arrest anywhere on earth?
Women from the CND, from Jeely Peace,
the greens, the health care workers, the ones
who fought for fair trade, for women's refuges,
equality, or welcome for the stranger,
all walked and sang, spoke out for truth.
Life and death are women's work,
and so was this. So is this always.

The voices of the past would say
'a whistling woman and a crowing hen
will drive the devil out of his den,'
as if she had no right to voice.
But life and death are women's work.
Signals will persist. There are voices.
There are lights.

The wrens are at the nest. He sings,
she calls, she whispers and he brings

grass and moss and leaves. She lines the cup
with hair and down and feathers.
She knows a living creature is a speaking being,
knowing herself by the one who listens,
by what he answers, by what we can say
when we know there is one who listens.
She lays her eggs, and waits.

Canto 4: Soil and Seed

Consider the grass of the field, consider it
in its idleness, growing and seeding
and dying and beautiful, free-loading
on the waste ground, not economically active
but growing, growing. After drought
it springs again, and when it dies
its leaves will rot and enrich the soil,
and it grows.

Consider the wide bluebell woods
the shelving depths of leaf litter,
the fungi and the mounded ant nests,
the blaeberries and bramble thickets
and the wrens singing against each other
flitting quietly, smoothly, between
the tangled ivy stems to find their nest.

Consider the bog, the layers of peat
metres deep, and the water held there,
and the moss, so many plants,
and the carbon trapped in the dead
still layers, not even rotting.
Consider the orchids and sundews,
the rushes and asphodel like a torch
and bog cotton's white wispy flags.
Consider the crickets, frogs and newts,
the adders and dragonflies.

Consider the moorland, its thin acid soil,
its heather and gorse. Consider the sheep
and the wild goats, the hare and the merlin,
the wild thyme and the blue squill,
rock rose and tormentil, and harebells
ringing in the cold thin wind of the hill.

Consider the clay, the silt, the chalk,
sand and peat, layers of leaf-mould, grass
and dung laid down, rotting and blending
while worm and beetle have their day.
Mycorrhizas among the roots exchange
sugar for phosphate, create a web of plants
unfurling for uncounted miles.

In the mossy nest, six warm white eggs
the size of a thumb-tip, ruby-freckled,
are safe beneath a wren's feathered breast.

Consider the pink helmets of balsam
nodding quietly in the river valleys.
Their angled pods explode and seven
hundred seeds can scud across the ground,
or drop into the stream. They spread
by air and water, crowding out
the lesser native plants, and banks collapse
as roots decay and lose their grip in winter.

How does a seed know, carried
on the feet, or in the shit of birds,
how to split the brittle seed case,
put out the small white neb of root,
hatch like a chicken in the warm dark?
Seeds that wait three thousand years
in an urn, in a tomb, in a clod,
that turn to the light, and sprout
as if no time at all had passed
must talk to the earth in language
more constant than the standing rocks.

Consider the human dreams
how they whisper in the brain's
quiet humus, and the small ideas
wriggle, digest, combine and mulch
the growing thought. Word-bees

waggle-dance from mouth to ear
with honey, pollen, venom. The roots
of language spread, to reach from mind
to hungry mind. Gods and demons
arise there, hide or burst full-grown
into the light, where they can find at last
good soil to prosper in.

The wren is whispering to the egg,
a small intimate song of love and hope
and the egg cracks, the chick wakes.
The chick taps on the shell. The parent bird
brings food. The eggshell breaks in answer.

Canto 5: A Web of Speaking Beings

'Even at its most fundamental level, life is innately dialectic.'
—Colin Tudge

Moon speaks to tide, and water
flows and ebbs across the world.
Light speaks to seed, and root
to water. Sun greets the flower
and the flower turns, and opens.
Flower calls the bee to nectar
and bees waggle and dance to bring
the whole hive to honey.

Two wrens flit with beaks full of ants,
caterpillars, moths, mosquitoes,
under the ivy branches. Their soft chirp
wakes the nestlings and their yellow
gapes open, begging, and are filled.

The curlew's flight upriver,
the tweedy feathers, skulking walk,
the curved bill probing, the liquid
fall of song as flooded field
becomes music—all this conversation
going on without a pause—
light between leaves, shadows,
water and leaves, *turadh*,
the cessation of rain, the clang
of wave, the blend of air and sun
and cloud-strewn skies all moving
loose and free, in dialogues of wing
and wind, of rain and earth.
And there is more to learn
than can be seen, and more
than can be taught.

All this keeps on going—
the growth and division,
waste and decay—
all this getting and killing,
eating and building and breaking
without our permission or oversight.
There's something here that doesn't know
the rules we think we know,
something more powerful
than we had imagined, a conversation
we are not privy to. We blame her
like we'd blame an avalanche.
Yet we know her like we know
the throb of our own hearts.

The whole earth is a web
of unheard conversations,
an open source technology
without firewall or password.
And we too are speaking beings,
our life is all in dialogues of blood
and thought and utterance
from conception to burial.
We learn by smell and touch
of our fingers on the stuff of earth,
then in the noise of our own chatter,
we forget, or choose to disregard.

The mind is tricksy and gullible;
the heart, though it wavers, is constant,
and what we think and feel
is as much a part of earth
and its continual transformation
as autumn or the phases of the moon.

We too are the universe grieving,
loving, building, fighting, forgiving.
We are less alienated than we think
from the earth that bore us.
Our work is earthly and our love
for children, parents, friends and strangers
is the earth's care for its own chicks.
Our language remembers and we speak
in words about her that are old
but still familiar—worn, almost nothing,
but ageless—field, hill, river, rock.

It is an April morning, and parent birds
sit on a nearby branch, cry 'jump!'
Six baby wrens jump, feather-fireworks,
exploding from the nest into green emptiness
and in a flap of wings opening, feeling the air,
they fly. Their wiry claws make purchase.
Agile among the twigs, they learn to hover,
to glide, and soon the only way
to tell them from their parents
is their gape as they line up to be fed.
And then they are gone.

Epilogue: In the Silence of Our Hearts

It must be here, it must be now,
for there is nowhere else, no later time.
And we must build with what we have,
start over among the wreckage,
love surviving like the wild horses
in the withered forests of Chernobyl.

A wren is singing
in the damp hush after the rain.
Between desire and action is insight,
a quiet emptiness where something like
the startling wake of poetry in my head
can happen, making new.

Among the wrecked buildings
abandoned in the heart of Govan
there are patches of tilled earth,
lavender and mint, two carrot plants,
a stand of potatoes. On the door
of an abandoned church, a poster—
classes for drummers, taekwondo,
English as a second language,
poetry for those who have the time
on a wet Friday morning, in all
the languages of earth.

In the silence, a wren is singing.

Notes

Haggards

The word haggard is derived from the OE 'hæg-geard 'hay-yard', but later meant a patch of land too small for cultivation where Irish peasants were allowed to grow crops for themselves. It is still used to indicate a patch of land left to run wild. The hedge schools of Penal times were held in such places.

'Who Knows'—the bbjs are 'boring brown jobs', birds that don't look interesting but are often the ones twitchers need to make up their life-lists.

'A Poem is'—the three musics in Gaelic tradition are 'the notes of joy' the 'notes of sorrow' and 'the notes of peace', often used for healing or sleep.

'Stand in the Light'—*canto jondo* is described as a fight to the death with misfortune; pibroch is a musical form for pipe music, not only laments as here; *nanha* is an Islamic lament for the fallen, and *tanakh* is a Hebrew form—the outcry of those who have lost everything.

Materia Medica

The study of plants for healing is referred to in old herbals as *materia medica*. My references are drawn from herbalists such as Gerard, Culpepper and Mrs Grieve, and there are some direct quotations.

'A Charm of Nine Haggard Herbs'—a local response to the Old English *Lacnunga*, A Charm of Nine Herbs, using some references drawn from it. Olwen in the Welsh tale *Culhwch and Olwen* was said to have been so beautiful that wherever she stepped, four white clovers sprang from her footprints.

'The Doctrine of Signatures'—a method of remembering the uses of plants by their appearance. Other teachers classified plants by their affinity with astrological ideas—thus herbs under the governance of Venus were warming, while those under Saturn were cooling.

'Molly-blobs'—Kingcups, or marsh marigolds.

The Wren in the Ash Tree

In folklore, the wren is the bringer of insight, and is credited with being one of the birds which brought fire to the earth—the others are the lark and the robin. Scientific information about wrens, and the lovely phrase, 'agile among the twigs' was drawn from *The Wren*, by Edward A. Armstrong and published by Collins in 1955.

'The Bird Who Brought the Fire': the epithets 'the druid's bird' etc are all traditional names for the wren in Celtic folklore.

'There are Lights': This is a quotation from the medieval theologian Duns Scotus.

'Valiant Women': The 'women I know' are my daughter Katherine Cameron, my husband's cousin Ann Nussey, who died in 2016, and my mother Ena Loughlin. The 'famous' women are:

Joanna Macy, environmental activist.
Elizabeth Warren, Senator resisting the regime of Donald Trump.
Mhairi Black, currently the youngest and most outspoken
    SNP MP.
Mary Barbour, leader of the Glasgow Women's rent strike.
Josephine Bacon, indigenous poet and activist in Canada.
Malala Yousafzai, activist for women's education, shot by the
    Taliban for going to school.
Dorothy Stang and Berta de Caceres, environmental activists in
    Central America, killed for their support for indigenous
    people.
Wangari Matthai, Kenyan feminist and environmentalist.
Mhairi Mhor, song-writer who documented the Highland
    Clearances.
Mary Brooksbank, author of the Jute Mill Song, inscribed on the
    wall of the Scottish Parliament.

Acknowledgements

Thanks are due to the editors of the following publications where many of these poems first appeared: *Poetry Scotland, The Write Angle* (Falkirk), *Eildon Tree*, the online magazines *And Other Poems, Ink Sweat and Tears, Jarmulla* and *InterlitQ*, the anthologies *Umbrellas of Edinburgh* (Freight Press), *Soundwaves* and *Landfall* (Federation of Writers, Scotland) and *The Physic Garden* (Palewell Press).

A long extract from *The Wren in the Ash Tree* appeared in *Dark Mountain* (9).

The poem 'Who Knows' was first published on the blog Seasonalight.

The poem 'Iris' was highly commended in the William Soutar Poetry Competition 2015.

I owe a special debt of gratitude to those good friends who have given me help support and feedback during the long gestation of *The Wren in the Ash Tree* and especially to Laura Fyfe, Janet Crawfurd, Sally Evans and the Burgh Poets, Anne Connolly, Roselle Angwin, Susan Richardson and Sheila Wakefield, my lovely publisher.

A NOTE ON THE TYPE

This book is set primarily in Clifford Pro,
a contemporary serif designed by Akira Koyabashi
and available in three weights and six fonts for various uses.
Clifford Pro performs excellently in digital environments
and is a sturdy, versatile and beautiful typeface
suited to a large variety of text work, including poetry.
It received a Certificate of Excellence in Type Design in 2000.

The ornaments are set in Eric Gill's Golden Cockerel,
with the exception of the wren silhouette at the start of section
three, which is modified from a photograph by Gerry Cambridge.